Omagh

Paintings by William M. Park
Text by Dr. Haldane Mitchell

First published by Cottage Publications,
Donaghadee, N. Ireland 2000.
Copyrights Reserved.
© Illustrations by William M. Park 2000.
© Text by Dr. Haldane Mitchell 2000.
All rights reserved.
No part of this book may be reproduced or
stored on any media without the express
written permission of the publishers.
Design & origination in Northern Ireland.
Printed & bound in Singapore.

ISBN 1 900935 20 1

The Author

Dr. C.J.H. Mitchell MB MICGP, was born in 1936 into a medical family in Omagh. Educated locally at the Model School and Omagh Academy he went on to Queen's University Medical School. He won Senior Colours for Rowing and represented the University at Henley Royal Regatta in 1957 and was a regular contributor to the Queen's Medical Magazine and the weekly student publication, Gown.

After completing his post-graduate year in the Royal Victoria Hospital in Belfast he joined his father in practice in Omagh in 1961, where he remained until retirement in 1996. His main interest now is historical photography, especially of the Omagh District, and he has published seven volumes of photographs on the subject over the past ten years.

The Artist

William M. Park was born in Scotland but made his home in Newtownstewart some twenty years ago. Having been an artist for ten years he paints mainly in watercolour but has also recently ventured into oils. As a member of the Watercolour Society of Ireland he has exhibited with the Royal Hibernian Academy and the Royal Ulster Academy.

Williams work shows an eye for detail and the dramatic use of light brings each scene to life with beautiful effect. His work is exhibited and sold through many galleries throughout Ireland and he is kept busy with private commissions as well as his exhibition work.

Contents

Beginnings

The glaciers of the Ice Age took millions of years to move slowly southwards across what is now known as Ireland. There were four of these Ice Ages until eventually Ireland appeared from beneath the retreating ice. Two large glaciers gave Ulster its deepest freeze of all, one covering Antrim and Down, and the other, via Foyle, covering the Sperrins and Omagh, breaking up over Neagh and Dungannon, igneous fragments were left in Tyrone.

25,000 years ago the fourth and last ice cap melted. Its thaw flooded the lowlands from Neagh to Erne, leaving mid-Tyrone as a lake of some proportion. Sand and gravel deposits built up and formed eskers. In 5000 BC the waters subsided and mid-Tyrone was left a soft soggy marsh.

The first people ever to come to Ireland settled around Larne and Coleraine (Mountsandel) about 6000 BC. Some of these people progressed westwards following the lakes and rivers and eventually ended up in Tyrone. They were nomadic in origin, their survival depending on their ability to find grass for their animals, or the reverse, finding animals to hunt and kill for food. Many descriptions of these people are given in the writings of folklore, but no-one really knows for certain what the early Tyrone man looked like.

The tools of these early people have been found all over this district, and in the region of the An Creagán Heritage Centre many stone circles and tombs remain for the visitor to see and discover how our ancestors worshiped the Moon, Sun, and other gods, as well as seeing the various methods they used to dispose of their dead over the millennia. Pottery, stones with hieroglyphics like ogham stones, and bronze implements are being found at regular intervals by builders and farmers. In 1999, when excavating at Newtownstewart Castle, a burial cist many thousands of years old (Bronze Age) was discovered. Many of the articles found are similar to those used by early inhabitants of France and further south in Europe, suggesting that the origin of early Irish man was southern European, between the Danube and the Rhine. Ethnologists classify them as Brittonic and Goidelic, or British and Gaelic. Archaeology is the best way to confirm these views.

Beginnings

In 2500 BC, a Breton flotilla bore the builders of the passage graves into the Irish Sea. In the Boyne Valley this group founded a thriving economy, and built three magnificent tombs, each covering more than an acre - New Grange, Dowth and Knowth. The portal tombs and passage graves around Carrickmore date from this period, with many more in other parts of the county, especially the Clogher Valley where Knockmany and Sess-Kilgreen still hold secrets of that little-known period in our history. Stone and mostly clay forts are widespread; many haven't been touched in centuries. The local townlands often got their names from the forts which dominated them. It is now almost impossible to detect primeval roots in our place names, because the Brittonic originals were nearly all Gaelicised after 350 AD, and Anglicised after 1350 AD.

For seven centuries, from c.300 BC, this area of Tyrone was extensively populated by the early Irish. However what made their ancestors move out of eastern Europe in a westerly direction towards Ireland those many years ago, must surely remain speculation for the historian. It could have been an earthquake or a revival of some ancient religion - we may never know.

The Ulster History Park at Cullion, Lislap, a short distance from Omagh on the Gortin Road, is one of the few sites in Ireland where you can follow the ancient Celt from his hide-covered hut, through the crannog with its dug-out canoes, via the motte and bailey and round towers, right up until Tudor times. The buildings are of authentic design and help the visitor to understand the lifestyle of the early Celt, how he lived, how he dressed and how he ate. Give it a visit and see for yourself.

Waterfalls have a fascination for many people, and the Sloughan Glen waterfall, after a spell of wet weather, is the most spectacular in the district. The water flows off flat, boggy heathland down into a fault in the rock with dramatic effect. Along the gorge on the approach to the waterfall, there is a great variety of ferns, mosses and fungi for the enthusiast to enjoy. Situated west of Drumquin (Droim Caoin) 'Pleasant ridge', this glen is in hilly, undulating countryside ideal for walkers attracted by its rugged beauty.

The area is full of interesting things to see, such as Kirlish Castle, built by Sir John Davies following the Plantation. It still contains several chimneys and a fine fireplace. Davies also built Castlederg Castle and a seven-mile road between the two castles in the straightest line possible, none of which remains today.

Approaching Drumquin from Omagh, on the left is quite a substantial early 19th century house, now a ruin, known as Burrell's Folly. It appears in all tourist guides, but little is known of its origin. History recalls that a Mr. Burrell with grandiose ideas built the house but, as is the case even today, could not pay for it and it was lived in by one of the Sproule families until recent times. They gave it the address 'Burrell's Folly', which can be seen on gifts presented to Upper Langfield Church.

Benedict Kiely, journalist, writer and broadcaster, who was born not a hundred miles from here, mentions Drumquin in several of his novels. But it was the poet Felix Kearney who penned the poem that is known worldwide;

"Drumquin you're not a city, but you're all the world to me".

Sloughan Glen
DRUMQUIN

"Through hills at the foot of Bessy Bell ... we come to Barons Court, Lord Abercorn's magnificent seat ... the great number of fine oaks and three long narrow lakes which ornament this place give it an air of great grandeur."

Coming from the east today, Daniel Beaufort would probably find his first impressions, written in 1786, only reinforced.

Baronscourt is situated in a sheltered and fertile valley. In 1612, following the original grant from James I, the Hamilton family built a fortified bawn or tower house - Derrywoone - a portion of which still stands about half a mile north of the present house. The family remained loyal to the Royal House of Stuart, and following the Battle of the Boyne, the 4th Earl of Abercorn fled to France with James II but, alas, the Earl died on the voyage. The anchor said to have belonged to the frigate Lausan on which they sailed can be seen embedded in the lawn in front of the Agent's house.

It was only with the succession in 1701 of the 6th Earl of Abercorn, a cousin from the branch which had remained Protestant, that the family fortunes began to revive. The present house was the idea of John James, 9th Earl and 1st Marquis of Abercorn. The 3rd Duke, born in 1869, followed his father and grandfather into politics, and is best remembered in the wider world as being the first Governor of Northern Ireland (1922-1945).

The House is not open to the public, but it is possible to drive around the estate on the public roads and enjoy some fine views of the house across the lake, the great variety of estate lodges such as Rock Cottage, and finally the estate church with its lych-gate. The rectory nearby was built in 1874 but is now in private ownership.

Baronscourt

Tucked away west of Omagh is the quiet village of Seskinore with no pubs or police station. It is set in an area of marsh and bog, hence the name- Sheskin Odhar.

Of Welsh origin, the Perry family was granted farm lands from Sir Audley Mervyn in 1662, and a first family house was built at Mullaghmore. The McClintocks from Argyll settled in Ireland in 1597, the family seat being at Newtown House, Co. Louth, and they came on the scene in 1781 when Mary Perry of 'Perrymount', Mullaghmore, married Alexander McClintock of Co. Louth, younger brother of John McClintock of Drumcar.

In 1862 they built a new home, designed by the famous architect Sir Charles Lanyon, about a mile from Perrymount, which they called Seskinore House. The McClintocks were very interested in field sports and the Tyrone Hunt, established in 1860, changed to the Seskinore Hunt in 1886. It met regularly at different venues, and only ceased to meet with the outbreak of the Second World War.

Seskinore Chapel of Ease, built in 1873 in the estate grounds a short distance from the 'big house', is a most picturesque little church. It was built as a private chapel for the family and their workers. The McClintock pew at the rear of the chapel is raised four inches above the level of all the other pews.

Colonel Jack was the last master of the house. He had served with the Royal Inniskilling Fusiliers and during the WW2, the U.S. Army had its headquarters at Seskinore House, the area referred to as 552nd Quartermaster Railhead Company. It was from here that supplies which had arrived by train at Beragh or Fintona were distributed to all other bases in the area. The soldiers came mainly from the 8th Infantry Division.

Seskinore

In 1818, a five year old boy called Thomas Mellon left Camphill, Mountjoy, with his parents and emigrated via the port of Derry to the United States. He laid the foundation for the development of the Mellon Bank in Pittsburgh, which has many business interests in America, for example, Gulf Oil.

A descendant, Dr. Matthew Mellon, acquired and refurbished his ancestral home and opened it to the public in 1968. The result is the Scotch Irish Trust of Ulster and the Ulster-American Folk Park, where many old buildings of the district have been relocated and rebuilt. One of these is the home of John Joseph Hughes from Augher, who emigrated in 1817, and became the first Roman Catholic Archbishop of New York. He built St. Patrick's Cathedral, and the high altar in Omagh's Sacred Heart Church was a gift from the parishioners of St. Patrick's to the Church in his memory.

The Folk Park contains several local buildings reconstructed in their original form and with a Mellon/Mountjoy connection. They include the old Presbyterian Church at Mountjoy in which Thomas Mellon worshiped as a boy, Castletown National School which was originally within one mile of the Park, while the original Post Office at Mountjoy, which dates back to 1861, has also been moved and fully equipped with all the original contents of the period, complete with Victorian letter-box.

The Park's library, which is open daily for all those who wish to study the Ulster-Scots-American link, contains a data-base of all who emigrated from the western counties of Ulster to the New World via the Port of Derry. A Master's Degree in Emigration Studies is run during the winter months in conjunction with Queen's University in Belfast.

Mellon Homestead
ULSTER AMERICAN FOLK PARK

The Strule Bridge on Drumragh Avenue was opened by the Duke of Abercorn in December, 1966, as Omagh's through-pass in order to relieve traffic congestion (it did then but doesn't now). Upstream is the confluence of the Camowen and Drumragh rivers which flow from the Carrickmore and Fintona areas respectively. Each autumn without fail these rivers flood some areas of the town. Look around you and imagine yourself on an island; well you would have been in 1913, 1929, 1954, 1969 and 1987.

   Looking downstream is probably the most photographed view of Omagh and its spires; against the setting sun, or floodlit at night, these spires are an imposing sight. The smaller of the three spires is that of St. Columba's Parish Church, built in 1777 by the Mervyn family. Bishop Knox added the tower and spire in 1820. The Church of the Sacred Heart was built between 1893 and 1899. A local merchant, Edward Boyle, and his sister contributed over one quarter of the cost of the building, which was in excess of £46,000. Its two spires are named after St. Patrick (212 feet) and St. Joseph (185 feet). The building has recently been completely restored and was re-opened following restoration on 30th August 1998. During the centenary year, the Chorus of the Kirov Opera from St. Petersburg in Russia performed Rachmaninov's Vespers on 12th June, 1999, a truly wonderful event for all those present.

This building replaced the only other chapel in Omagh in Brook Street to St. Peter and St. Paul, built in 1829.

Omagh Spires

The confluence of the Camowen and Drumragh rivers to form the Strule was from the beginning of time a very important fording point, and one to be closely guarded. The general opinion is that it was Art O'Neill who set up a stronghold here in 1440, building a castle near the ford and calling the town Omey. He also had a look-out post on the site occupied by the Courthouse today.

The Planters of 1609 built their fortified house and bawn in marshy land below the town where Gortmore Gardens is built today. At the beginning of the 20th century it was said that wooden piles, thought to be the remains of Edmund Leigh's castle of the early 17th century, were visible at low water during the summer mouths. Fire and battle over the centuries destroyed original settlements, the last fire being in 1742 when only a dozen or so houses remained.

In 1768, Omagh became the county town of Tyrone. A gaol was built at the top of the High Street, and an infirmary with 29 beds in Market Street in 1796, the latter being older than the Royal Victoria Hospital in Belfast. The gaol, built in the 1790s, was opened on its present site in 1804 and finally closed in 1904. This left the site vacant for the Courthouse, which looks down the High Street like a Palladian mansion. Cork architect, John Hargrave, was in County Tyrone designing Favor Royal for the Moutrays, and he was commissioned to design the Courthouse, which was built in 1814 and added to by W.J. Barre in 1863.

Sadly, Hargrave never saw the finished building as he was drowned in a sailing accident off Cork. The niche in the north wall in George's Street contained a periwigged figure of Justice, removed in the 1960s during renovations and never replaced.

Dobbins Shopfront
GEORGES STREET

The three main O'Neill strongholds in the area between 1431 and 1609 were at Omagh, Dungannon and Castletown - Fintona. The modern name Fintona dates from the 17th century, and is derived from the original Irish 'Fionntamhnach' meaning 'the fair watered land'.

In 1619 the O'Neill Castle at Castletown formed the site of the bawn and house built by John Leigh, who had received a grant of 2,000 acres from James I. Following 200 years under O'Neill rule and a further 50 in the control of the Leighs, Fintona passed in 1668 into the possession of the Eccles family - through Gilbert Eccles (1602-1694) of Shannock in South Fermanagh.

The original house, with the Ecclesville coat of arms above the door, was built by Gilbert Eccles' son Charles, in 1703. The house was altered and extended by Daniel Eccles in 1795 with the addition of fireplaces and plasterwork said to be of the finest in the district at that time. Charles erected an elaborate stone tablet to his father's memory. Bearing the family coat of arms, crest and motto, 'Nec Animus Deficit', it can still be seen on the tower of the old ruined church at Castletown. The inscription (in capitals in the original Latin) translates as follows:-

"This cenotaph Charles Eccles of Fintona in County Tyrone, gentleman, had made in memory of his father, Gilbert Eccles of Shannock in County Fermanagh,

gentleman, who honourably lived and dutifully died on the 6th of the kalends of August, in the year of the Lord 1694 in the 92nd year of his age. Remember Death."

The estate was sold in 1961 on the death of its last resident, the flamboyant Raymond Browne-Lecky. An actor by profession, Raymond and his friends performed plays in his 'in-house' theatre. Dressed in his own inimitable style, he could be easily recognised when chauffeur-driven to town in his large two-tone Austin 16.

Fintona

When the linen industry expanded throughout Ulster, mills were constructed to cope with the local demand. This was the case at Mullaghmore in an area owned by the Stack family; an entrepreneurial businessman named Donnelly built a mill with a bleach green nearby. It got its water power from a weir across the river Camowen at a spot now called the 'Lovers' Retreat', a public park owned by Omagh District Council and first acquired in the 1920s. The name comes from the fact that a weeping willow stood in the middle of the park and, when in full leaf, young lovers could retreat beneath its branches and not be seen!

Nearby the Stack family home, Mullaghmore House, remains today, with a unique Millennium attraction in the garden; this is in the form of a Viking warrior sculptured in timber by the owner, Louis Kelly. The family built a fine Jacobean mansion further along the Old Mountfield Road in 1886. This was called Knocknamoe Castle, designed by Sir Charles Lanyon. Sadly, the house has fallen victim of the present troubles.

The Old Mill has gone, but the lade which was channelled under the Killyclogher Burn, and some of the sluice gates which controlled it, are still there. The lade can be followed to where it rejoins the river Camowen at Donnelly's Bridge (1840) on the main road to Cookstown, and named after the man who built the mill.

The Killyclogher burn which flows into the river Camowen at the Lovers' Retreat has its origin in Glenhordial mountain, a short distance away, and the original source of Omagh's first piped water supply. The burn was always a great area for children to play on a summer's day with nets, jam-jars, or just paddling about enjoying themselves.

LOVERS' RETREAT
MULLAGHMORE

According to legend, when Cromwell's troops left Omagh via the Cannon Hill Road, they fired their cannons at the Old Parish Church of Drumragh and destroyed it. Although rebuilt and used until 1777, it is now a ruin. Above a gentle bend of the Drumragh River is the old graveyard, which is the oldest burial ground in the district. The first Parish Priest, Terence McCawell of Drumragh Parish, is buried here. It was he who built the first Catholic chapel in the district at St. Mary's, Drumragh, in 1763. A few miles further on is the rectory of the parish at Tattyreagh Glebe, built in the late 18th century, with the much older and well-preserved Black Fort nearby.

Two miles to the west is the hamlet of Ballynahatty, one time home to local landlord Audley Mervyn. When Omagh was burned accidentally on 4th May, 1742, it was his intention to rebuild the town on this site. The area did have quarterly fairs in the 19th century, and there were two pubs and a small prison for offenders - it is still to be seen. Little of the Presbyterian Church of Ballynahatty remains, and the school has gone. The hill beside it is still called Castle Hill, but nothing remains of the house.

Vincentia Rodgers (1790-1835), who became a poetess of some note, was born here, as was Bishop Francis Kelly (1812-1889) in nearby Drudgeon. He later became Bishop of Derry, and was responsible for the building of St. Eugene's R.C. Cathedral and other ecclesiastical buildings in the city. At nearby Baronagh, disturbed ground is said to be the burial place of the victims of the famine in this area.

When others join the festive ring
The wildest love meed let me bring.
With sweetest flowers of early spring
To deck thy raven brow, Anna.

'Anna' by Vincentia Rodgers (1790-1835)

Old Drumragh Graveyard

Six Irish miles from Omagh is Sixmilecross. Established in 1634, it is a quiet little village; tucked away in Ulster heartland and is said to be the geographical centre of Ulster.

St. Michael's Church of Ireland church at the lower end of the village has a stained-glass window commemorating the Dunlap family, one of whom was John Dunlap, who printed the United States Declaration of Independence. In the vestry is a window etched with the signatures of all the clergy that have served this parish to date. Nearby at Dunmoyle the castle built by a family named Jeffcock in the 1830's, and later extended by Colonel Deane Mann. The last resident was his son-in-law, the eminent public servant Sir John Ross, who is buried in the church graveyard. He was born on 13th July, 1888, and died on 31st July, 1958. Only the attractive drinking trough opposite the main gate remains.

The best-known name in this area is that of the Reverend William Forbes Marshall, BA, LL.B, DD, MRIA, Presbyterian Minister from 1915 to 1928. Often referred to as the Bard of Tyrone, his poems covered all aspects of life which he witnessed from day to day as part of his duties going round his parish. Many of the places referred to in his poems still remain, but the characters have gone. For example, the Fairy Hill at Junk's Bridge, Bernish Glen, and Tullyneil. He also wrote several books. 'Planted by a River', a historical novel published in 1949, is the best-known. Many of his most popular poems weren't written until he went to live and work in Castlerock after 1928. A great tragedy in his life was the loss of his Ulster Scots Dictionary manuscript, which was destroyed by his golden retriever pup and never rewritten. He died on 25th January, 1959, and is buried in his beloved Tyrone.

Sixmilecross

Termon Rock or Carrickmore was the site of an early monastery associated with St. Columba. From the height, one can look down on the remains of the mediaeval parish church, below the Roman Catholic church. There are small graveyards nearby for unbaptised children, suicides and slain men. All such unfortunates, dying without the Last Rites of the Church, were buried in unconsecrated ground.

The area, at some 600 feet, has wonderful views of the surrounding countryside and is steeped in ancient history. Chiefs, like the McKeaghneys and the McGurks, fought over the area until in the 1600s. They were the erenaghs or stewards of the church lands and Termonmaguirke - the Parish of the McGurks, is the name used today for the eighteen townlands round the village.

In 'A Topographical Directory of Ireland' (1837) Samuel Lewis states:-

"Adjoining the village are the picturesque remains of the old Church of Termon, the side walls and eastern gable of which are nearly perfect; the windows are of beautiful design, and the building appears to have been an elegant specimen of the decorated English style. The cemetery is still a favourite burial place for Roman Catholic parishioners; nearby is a separate burial place for children, and within a quarter of a mile is one exclusively for women."

The women's graveyard which 'no living woman or dead man may enter' is still frequently mentioned.

A short distance south of the village stands the hill of Dunmisk, where it is said James II encamped on his return from Derry in 1689, and from where he continued his journey south to the Boyne.

Loughmacrory Lodge, a Regency-style lodge looking west over the lough, was the last home of the Stewarts in this area and is now in private ownership. The Parish Church of St. Columba contains the burial vault of the Stewart family, and the interior has some delightful oak panelling.

Carrickmore

The village of Plumbridge, affectionately known as 'the Plum' by the locals, sits astride the Glenelly river as it rushes down from the mountains to join the Owenkillew and eventually the Mourne. This is the ideal starting point for ramblers, mountain climbers or motorists to tour this beautiful area, which has so much to offer the visitor.

To the west is Corrick Glen with the remains of its 15th century Abbey of the Third Order Franciscans. To the north, the road climbs steeply past St. Joseph's School with probably the best view of any school in the country. To the east, the Butterlope Glen at 800 feet is popular with walkers and has the remains of five stone circles.

The road east out of 'the Plum' passes Glenelly Presbyterian Meeting House, with Campbell's mill nearby, and on to Cranagh, where the Heritage Centre tells the story of gold-mining in the local hills - you can even try your hand at panning for some in the local streams. The beauty of the hills all around is made more magnificent with the effect of the clouds moving by and allowing the sun through, making it a paradise for the painter.

On to Sperrin itself, a crossroads that comes down from Barnes Gap and up between Sawel (2240 feet) and Dart gives the visitor easy access for exploring. The Ulster Way passes this route, taking in a selection of the highest hills for the energetic.

Plumbridge has a fine chapel built in 1896 from red rock-freed sandstone. Upper Badoney Parish Church, originally built in 1784, sits in the valley, whilst at Cranagh is the Chapel of St. Patrick, built in 1897.

Plumbridge

Approach Gortin via the main road or the scenic route by the lakes above the village and you will be astonished by the beauty of the village nestling in the Owenkillew valley below, with the grandeur and changing colour of the mountains all around.

Beltrim Castle is of Plantation origin, when William Hamilton erected a house and bawn on a steep bank of the river. The river was diverted at one point to encompass more of the estate and also for protection. The remains of the castle form part of the garden wall, and most of the large house to the west was built between 1785 and 1820. It has a classical farmyard of the period. In spring, the rhododendrons make a wonderful sight as the front garden falls away steeply. The Hamiltons married into the Coles of Florencecourt and became Cole-Hamilton.

The Parish Church of Lower Badoney (1856) in the village contains many fine memorials to the family, and two unusual stained-glass windows by J.B. Capronnier of Brussels (1872) of The Baptism of Christ and The Last Supper. The property remained in the possession of the Cole-Hamiltons until 1929. During the Second World War, the Americans occupied some of the estate, which was originally of some 4,000 acres; today it is 400 acres.

St. Patrick's Roman Catholic Church is at the east end of the village (1898-1902) and it imposes itself on the landscape. The foundation stone was laid by the Most Reverend J.K. O'Doherty, Bishop of Derry, on 9th October, 1898. The Presbyterian Church, built in 1843, is tucked away on the right-hand side of the main street. The first three ministers served for over one hundred years between them: the Reverend Matthew Logan, the Reverend Adam White, and the Reverend Smith, who died in July, 1981.

Gortin

With thanks to Mr & Mrs Blakiston-Houston

At Rousky (marshy land) in the heart of the glens, there is a very well preserved sweat-house. This was the original Irish sauna, where folk with aches and pains were placed in a stone building which had been preheated by a fire of turf. After a period in the sweat-house, the patient emerged only to be fully immersed in a local stream or a barrel of cold water.

The glen men looked after their religion, and this region has a surprising number of churches for such an isolated population. The Roman Catholic Church of St. Mary's was originally a thatched church built in 1800 by the Reverend Bernard O'Neill. It was the first post-penal church built in this area. It was improved in 1882 by the Reverend Peter McGeown, and again in 1958.

At Crockatanty there was a small Presbyterian church (now disused) built by a John Browne on his farm in the early 1890s so that he and those of his faith would not have to travel to far distant places of worship. A few of the remaining pewter communion vessels are in the church in Gortin.

Greenan Church of Ireland church nearby is built on a site given by A.W. Cole-Hamilton, it was consecrated on 6th June, 1859. Greenan (sunny situation) originated as a wattle and daub hut in the 17th century. The present structure was built by the four Colhoun brothers from Lenamore, who travelled each day on foot and moved the materials needed to build the church by horse and cart. A wander round the churchyard, set in this very remote part of Ulster, is recommended; observe the tombstones - three-quarters have the name 'Ballantine'.

Today, Rousky is a centre for Irish traditional music, and folk travel from miles around to the gatherings.

Sweat-house
Rousky

McCullaghs' prize-winning hostelry stands at the crossroads that lead in and out of the glens. The locals at a time had their cattle mart across the road, while the Post Office at Sheskinshule is just round the corner, looked after by the Devlins who used to bring their goods by horse and cart from Cookstown and Draperstown.

The area contains approximately two hundred known prehistoric sites, including the Beaghmore (big area of birches) stone circles. Above Crock old school is one of the most fascinating, the Dun Ruadh (Ringfort), a series of stone circles and cairns of Bronze Age origin, 2000-1000 BC. In the townland of Aughascribba (furrowed field) stands a fine example of an Ogham stone, with its markings clearly visible. At the nearby An Creagán Heritage Centre, the visitor can get information on all the excavations done in the area. The Centre itself is interesting from an architectural point of view in that it is built in the shape of an ancient stone circle.

Glenlark a little further on, has a history all of its own with respect to Gaelic-speaking, hand-sewn garments made from wool, and traditional music. This was one of the last Gaelic-speaking areas in Tyrone.

Further on past Crock is Broughderg, where the chapel of 1876 has been replaced by a new building on the crest of the hill. Our Lady of the Wayside is the last work of Father Seamus Shields, who was known as the 'entrepreneurial priest' because of the fine works he carried out in the parishes in which he worked. He is laid to rest here, not far from a commemoration of the Crucifixion - a fine place to stop and meditate, and gather one's thoughts.

Ogham Stone

GREENCASTLE

Mountfield is situated six miles east of Omagh. The area was acquired by Dublin judge, Sir William McMahon, in 1846 on the sale of the Blessington estates. It was his intention to found a town here to rival Omagh. He first built Fecarry Lodge, and later a descendant built Mountfield Lodge, which had one of the first water turbines in Ireland, worked from water from Mountfield Lake above. It worked two mills as well as lighting the house.

The tiny Church of Ireland Chapel of Ease, above the village, was built in 1826 at a cost of £830, with a grant from the Board of First Fruits, and has a delightful two-stage tower. The Catholic Chapel is of more recent construction. Alice Milligan, the poetess, once lived in the Old Rectory in the village. Loughmacrory Lodge, once the shooting lodge for Ballygawley Park and home of the Stewart family, is now in private ownership.

The area is noted for its sand and gravel pits, which extend over to Loughmacrory. There are a great many lakes of various sizes in the area. Lough Fingrean, the largest of the lakes, supplies Omagh with its water supply on the east, whilst Lough Braden supplies the water on the west side of the town.

There are many beautiful walks around Lough Fingrean and Loughmacrory where one can enjoy complete solitude. This area also has several prehistoric sites of note Creggandevesky court tomb just west of Lough Mallon, and one of the earliest-discovered graves, Cregganconroe court tomb; both are well signposted. A gold lunula found rolled up under a stone at Cregganconroe has been in the Royal Irish Academy since 1900.

Scalp Hill is where, on the first Sunday in August, children would pick bilberries and the young men would show their athletic prowess to the assembled crowd of onlookers.

Fernagh Cottage
Mountfield

Lis na Mallacht or 'the cursed fort' was purchased by John Buchanan of Omagh from Sir Hugh Stewart in 1828.

The 1833 Ordnance Survey map shows extensive planting around the house, which was then called 'Millbank'. By the time of the 1854 map, there is evidence of more planting and formal gardens. The oldest beech trees on the property predate the present house, the oldest part of which was built between 1790 and 1820. Margaret Scott constructed three linked greenhouses along the south-facing wall in the 1890s, which extended 86 feet from the potting shed to the end of the terrace and which survived until the mid-1980s. On their demolition, seven brick-lined recesses or niches were discovered in the surviving retaining wall - a bee wall of an earlier period which would have provided honey for the household before sugar was commercially available.

With the exception of Mullaghmore House on the Old Mountfield Road, Lisnamallard is almost certainly the oldest residential property, outside the town, in the Omagh urban area. Charles Scott of W & C Scott - Excelsior Mills - bought the house in 1887; it had lain empty for some years, and his wife Margaret later wrote of having to be accompanied by a man with a scythe when she came to investigate the garden before she brought it and the house under control. It is thought that this was the second dwelling-house in Omagh to have central heating with radiators in 1911, the first public building to be centrally heated being the Courthouse.

The house was requisitioned by the military authorities during the Second World War for the Americans, who left two pieces of G.I. art as murals - one, a tasteful reclining nude. The house was acquired from the Scott family in September, 1997, by Omagh District Council as an extension to adjacent parkland for the people of Omagh.

Lisnamallard

Dromore (Droim Mor) is surrounded by townlands beginning with Meen and Drum called after the many drumlins in the district. Dromore is overlooked by Greenan mountain (864 feet), the highest point in the area. It is easily accessed (with permission) with fine views of Lower Lough Erne in the west to Omagh in the east. The original town owes its origin to William Hamilton of Aughlish, who gave a grant of land (Mullinacross) in 1767 to the Stewarts and Humphreys to develop the town.

The site has a connection with Clogher, for the Abbey site was originally that of a nunnery founded by St. Patrick for St. Cettumbria. Cinnia, daughter of the royal house of Clogher at Rathmore, was sent to Cettumbria here at Dromore for her novitiate; thus Dromore had the first nun in Ireland.

The once ivy covered church ruin at the top of the village is that of a Protestant church built in 1694, most likely on the site of a plantation building. There are many interesting grave stones in the graveyard. The imposing new church of St. Davog (1987) dominates the skyline, while the old church of St. Dympna (1835) is behind the hill out of sight. A square bell-tower with cupola stands at a higher level, once used to call the faithful to prayer.

Holy Trinity Parish Church, built in 1957 by A. T. Marshall, replaces one of 1839. The tower is from Aughentaine Castle, Fivemiletown, which was being demolished at that time. Opposite is the large Regency-style rectory, built around 1830 by the Reverend H. Lucas St. George.

In this parish, a survivor of the Great Famine was one of its most remarkable local characters of the 19th century. The Reverend James Reid Dill (1814-93), was from a noted Donegal family from Springfield in Fanad and was the local Presbyterian clergyman.

DROMORE

It was only after the Great Famine that roads of any quality were built in Ireland, to be followed by the greatest revolution of all - the railways; had they come sooner, the famine may not have been such a tragic part of our history.

Omagh's railway history extends over a period of 113 years. The first line linked Derry with Omagh in 1852. The 34 miles of track to Omagh took seven years to construct. The pioneer of railways, George Stephenson, and his son Robert surveyed the line running along the Rivers Foyle, Mourne and Strule. The line reached Enniskillen in 1854, with one little branch line from Fintona Junction, worked by the now famous horse van.

Meantime, the Dundalk and Enniskillen Railway Company was forging ahead with a line from the east, which began at Dundalk in 1845. It eventually reached Enniskillen in 1858 - taking thirteen years to construct sixty-two miles of single track. Omagh had a direct link with Dublin via Enniskillen and Clones.

In 1862, the above two companies amalgamated to form the Irish North Western Railway, known affectionately as 'the Irish North'. The Ulster Railway Company had leased a line from the Portadown, Dungannon and Omagh Junction Railway Company. This line arrived in Omagh in 1861. It had its own goods station in Irish Town via Omagh Market Branch. In 1876, the local and several other Northern railway companies amalgamated to become the Great Northern Railway Company. The Company remained intact until 1953 when its southern line became Coras Iompair Eireann, whilst north of the border the Great Northern Railway Board (later the Ulster Transport Authority) was formed.

Railway history ended in Omagh in February, 1965, when the U.T.A. closed the line from Portadown to Derry via Omagh. The town has never really recovered from the loss of its railway connections to many parts of Ireland.

Station House
BERAGH

When you approach Omagh, its spires suggest the presence of churches, thus giving the impression that this is a town with a religious background. This is quite true as history suggests an abbey in Omagh as early as 792 AD, situated in the Abbey Street/Derry Road area of the town however nothing now remains of the Abbey of Gortmore.

This area now has the remains of Omagh Gaol, which closed in 1904. The gaol was originally located at the top of High Street on the site of the present Courthouse, which was built between 1814 and 1822. The gaol on the present site started in 1790, opened in 1804 and was of dual gender with approximately 145 inmates. Their weekly allowance of provision was four stone of potatoes, seven and a half pounds of oatmeal, and seven pints of new milk per prisoner.

The last public execution to take place there was in 1860 when John Holden was hanged for the murder of a policeman. However, by far the best known inmate of Omagh gaol must be Montgomery, who was hanged at 8 a.m. on 26th August, 1873 for the murder of the Newtownstewart bank cashier, William Glass. Glass was killed in his office on 29th June, 1871 when a file was stuck in his neck. The case caused a sensation principally because his murderer, Thomas Hartley Montgomery, was his friend and a police inspector, who initially investigated his own crime. He underwent two trials in which the jury disagreed, but fresh evidence of

Montgomery's financial pressure, partly due to gambling debts, helped persuade the third jury of his guilt in just twenty minutes. On the morning of his execution there was a severe thunderstorm, and this led many local inhabitants to believe that Heaven had sent a sign that an evil-doer was being justly punished.

James Street
OMAGH

The Blessington Estate of some 40,000 acres stretched from Newtownstewart to Mountfield at its height. It contained a large acreage of forest, the planting of which was overseen by John McEvoy from 1791.

The Estate was sold in or around 1846 when the owners fell on hard times, to a wealthy Omagh family named Spiller who acquired some 400 acres which included Rash House. It was the original shooting lodge of Old Mountjoy and built by the Gardiners, part of the Stewart-Blessington dynasty in this part of Tyrone. At that time they also owned several big houses and streets in the City of Dublin; for example, Gardner Street, Gloucester Street, King's Inn Street, and many more.

Lislimnaghan Parish Church, 'the fort of the little bare place', was built because of tragedy in the Spilliers family, Jane Spiller had three sons, all of whom died before herself.-

John - died 1st April 1823 aged 5 years
Robert - died 10th March 1843 aged 22 years
George Thomas - died 1st April 1859 aged 35 years.

The church was built by Jane in 1862 at a cost of £1,600 in memory of her beloved son George Thomas Spiller. On Jane's death the estate came into the Ellis family through will and family connections with Jane's sister.

The Rash House acreage was increased by the present owner. The carved lions by the door come from Clonleigh House, Lifford, home of a branch of the present family.

Lislimnaghan Church

The last great fire in Omagh was in May, 1742, when a chambermaid, careless in discarding lighted coals, accidentally burnt the town to the ground in a matter of hours. Following this, the prosperous merchants decided that it was safer to move out of town and build their new houses in private secluded sites such as Glencree. Built in the late 1700s, the house has been modernised but the quaint gate-lodge remains untouched.

The famous Henry Grattan, the Irish and English lawyer and politician who worked, for the emancipation of the Irish cause, had his roots in Cappagh, where his grandfather, Patrick Grattan, was installed in 1671, and his father, William Grattan, after ordination preached here from 1703 to 1719.

In 1622 Gervase Walker, son of an Englishman, was installed in Cappagh Parish Church and later resigned in favour of his son George. Both Walkers were grandfather and father of the Reverend George Walker, the defender of Derry in 1688/89.

Dunmullan old church and graveyard lies a little further on; this is a pre-Reformation church of the late 16th century. It is situated on top of a hill with the backdrop of the foothills of the Sperrins beyond. A famous monument in the transepts depicts a coat of arms which includes a sow and a litter of piglets. History relates that a local family had to leave the district in a hurry during the 1641 rebellion, and a baby was left behind. When the family felt it safe to return they found the baby still alive, having been suckled by the sow along with her own piglets.

Gate Lodge
GLENCREE

On the west-facing slopes of Bessy Bell (Slieve Trim) is the first electricity-producing wind farm in County Tyrone. More ancient Neolithic tombs may be seen on the slopes and also on Mary Gray, the mountains whose charming names are thought to commemorate two sisters who fled here from Derry to escape the plague in the 15th century. The three lakes known as Catherine, Fanny and Mary are named after three other sisters, daughters of the last Marquess of Abercorn.

In the valley below lies the quiet village of Mountjoy, just off the main Omagh to Newtownstewart Road. In various ways it has served this thriving farming population for many years. It once boasted the most comprehensive country store in the district that of the late Harry O'Doherty, whose family (originally from Inishowen) had traded here for over 120 years. They blended their own tea, made their own meal - Strule Valley Oatmeal - and did a big business in egg-marketing.

Mountjoy had its own railway halt on the GNR line, with a small siding to serve the store and the creamery nearby. On excursion days to the seaside at Bundoran, the train would come out from Omagh to collect the excited travellers; for many in those days this might be their only day out in the entire year.

The Presbyterian Church of the Crossroads at Mountjoy was built in the 17th century (no trace remains). It is known that a church existed here in 1791. The present church was built in 1871 and bears a striking resemblance to Lislimnaghan Church of Ireland nearby. The Mountjoy church recently acquired a bell for the bellcote which previously didn't have one.

Windmills on Bessy Bell

When the railway came to Omagh in 1852, the traffic generated in the town necessitated the widening of John Street on its lower side. The junction of John Street and Church Street had a hostelry called Hollands, and on the gable wall was painted 'The First and Last'. This was with respect to the railway station. Today, the hostelry known as Sally O'Briens contains many artifacts from Harry O'Doherty's shop at Mountjoy. It also has one of Omagh's three popular night-spots, 'The Eden'.

John Street and James Street are named after members of the Galbraith family. It was in the 1630s that John Galbraith, who had moved to Kiladroy from Longford in the early 1600s, became an agent for the Earl of Belmore. This led to him acquiring land for himself in the Parish of Drumragh, and at Clanabogan where a later member of the family built in 1809 a large house called 'New Grove' which still stands today. In Slaters Directory of 1860 Samuel Galbraith J.P. and his brother John were listed as lessors of several houses and tenements in High Street, James Street, Kevlin Road and other parts of the town of Omagh.

Inspired by the beauty of the surrounding countryside, Tyrone has produced a number of noted poets and songwriters. One such, the prolific song-writer, Jimmy Kennedy, was born in Pretoria Terrace on 20th July, 1902. Jimmy was involved with the writing of over 2,000 songs, and in 1971 he was awarded the Ivor Novello Prize for his outstanding contribution to British music. The list of songs is endless, but the best-known include: Red Sails in the Sunset; The Isle of Capri; The Teddy Bears' Picnic and, the most-recorded of all, South of the Border Down Mexico Way.

Sally O'Briens
JOHN STREET

Station Island in Lough Derg with St. Patrick's Purgatory dates back to the time of St. Patrick. Nearby is Saint's Island, of which St. Davog, Patrick's disciple, was the first abbot. The river Derg begins its course in the lough and flows gently through the tree and heather-covered terrain of Tyrone, passing Killeter, Castlederg and Ardstraw, into the fertile lowlands of the valley, before entering the Mourne at Smith's Bridge below Newtownstewart.

On its way it passes through land once owned by the Ferguson family and later the Alexanders of Caledon. They owned the Lough House, which was their summer residence being close to the lough for fishing, and Killeter Forest, planted since the 1950s. Also nearby was their main residence in Aghyaran, the Derg Lodge, which was used to entertain shooting parties on the nearby Corgories.

The Reverend William Alexander, Rector of Termonamongan, 1950-1955, resided at the Lodge with his wife, Cecil Frances, best remembered for her hymn-writing. She wrote over 150 in all, and 'There is a Green Hill Far Away' is her best-known, and attributed to every area in which she lived. The Reverend Alexander eventually became Archbishop of Armagh and Primate of All Ireland. The Parish Church, situated at Woodside, Killeter, was built in 1822, consecrated 1827, and dedicated to St. Bestius, who cannot he identified with any degree of certainty.

The town of Castlederg on the banks of the Derg, serves an important and thriving agricultural area of Tyrone - the most westerly. Castlederg was unique insomuch as it had its own tramway to Victoria Bridge, and hence the G.N.R. from July 1884 until the rail strike of 1933. It carried a lot of cattle, and ran along the roadside.

Castlederg

The Victorian garden village of Sion Mills (Sidhean - a fairy mound) is well-known for its linen industry, but its architecture is quite unique.

It was in 1835 that the Herdmans from Scotland adapted what had been a flour mill owned by the Abercorns of Baronscourt to a flax-spinning mill with the help of water from the River Mourne, with eventually a turbine of eighty horse power which drove eight thousand spindles.

The imposing Victorian mill with its chimney still stands, with its sixteen bays long and four storeys high. It was designed in the 1840s by W.H. Lynn of Belfast. The original mill employed upwards of 700 people, 500 of whom were women; the present day modern Mourne Mill employs only a fraction of that number.

The Herdmans set about building the ideal industrial village for themselves and their workforce. It was to designs of Emerson Tennent Herdman's brother-in-law, the London architect W.F. Unsworth, that most of the main striking buildings can be attributed.

The family home, Sion House, was built in 1846 and redesigned in 1884. The gate-house has been refurbished, and the fine old stables await the same treatment. The house itself sadly, is in a state of decline. The Church of the Good Shepherd (Church of Ireland) was built in 1909. Designed by Unsworth, it has an unusually

elaborate Italianate Romanesque style, modelled on a church in Pistoia. The memorial in the form of a sarcophagus stands in front of the church and is to Brigadier-General Ambrose St. Quentin Ricardo, a member of the family remembered for his part in setting up the U.V.F. in this area of Tyrone during the Home Rule Crisis.

The Recreation Hall (1882) and School (1899) are Unsworth's work, whilst the Catholic Church of St. Teresa (1963) designed by Patrick Haughey, is dominated by a long slate sculpture of The Last Supper by Oisin Kelly.

Sion Mills

The District Lunatic Asylum or, as it is called today, the Tyrone and Fermanagh Hospital, must be the most imposing building in the district. It owes its existence to the gentry of Tyrone and Fermanagh who came together to make their claim for a hospital in the West. Two were granted to Ulster in 1817, one in Belfast and one in Armagh. It was in 1847 that the First Warrant was issued, but this had no connection with the famine that was then raging.

The original site was 26 acres; the stone came by horse and cart from a quarry at Lack. William Farrell was the architect. The cost was £41,407.12s.2d. The first insurance was £7.10s.0d. The initial design was for 300 patients.

On 3rd May, 1853, the first 36 patients from Omagh Gaol and Omagh Workhouse arrived. The first name listed was Brian Corr of Omagh. Two years later, on 31st March, 1855, there were 142 patients from Tyrone and 43 from Fermanagh. John West, M.D., an Edinburgh graduate, was the first Resident Medical Superintendent. In 1860, the first mention of padded cells and strait-jackets being used. The boundary wall had only been built six feet high, and any athletic patient could have easily escaped. However, a three feet ditch was dug on the inside the whole way round, effectively making the wall nine feet in height from the inside.

By 1873 the hospital farm had increased to 72 acres. No ploughing was done thirty-six acres were under the spade. There were two horses, twenty-seven cows and thirty-one pigs - the stock was increasing.

The patient population reached its peak in 1959 with numbers then at 1,116, making it the largest hospital of its kind outside Purdysburn. With massive cut-backs in recent years, the hospital has gone full-circle, with the patient population today down to 215.

Tyrone & Fermanagh Hospital

The Rope Walk in the late 1800s was the left-hand side of the Brookmount Road, so-called because of the ropeworks that existed there for the production of various calibres of rope. Tucked away in the trees opposite the Brookmount Road is one of Omagh's architectural treasures, the Loreto Convent.

Setting up educational establishments in Omagh in the middle of the 19th century was extremely difficult, and Omagh at that time was certainly considered an out-of-the-way place for most. The Sisters of Charity came from Derry, took one look, and left! Father Manasses O'Kane, the then incumbent of the Parish of Drumragh, invited the Loreto Sisters from Rathfarnham in Dublin to come and set up a school in Omagh. They duly arrived in 1855 by stage coach. Six women under Mother Feticitas Murray set about the job of educating the young women of the parish, and after several different homes, starting at 8 George's Street, the Harkin family donated the grounds where the present Convent stands.

It was built in 1859 to a design by Hadfield and Goldie, at a cost of £11,000. The design is French Gothic, and has three storeys. The chapel was a later addition, with stained-glass windows by Mayer of Munich, and its own two-keyboard pipe organ by the Positive Company of Dublin. Because of the district it had to support and the lack of suitable transport, boarding was introduced before the turn of the century and continued until the 1970s. The new National School was built in the grounds adjoining the Brookmount Road in 1894.

The bodies of Mother Feticitas and her friends, Imelda McGlade, Berchmans Hermans, Mary Anastasia, Frances Martin and De Pazzi Donnelly, now lie at peace in the vault in a quiet area of the Convent grounds.

Loreto Convent
Omagh

In the quiet of the countryside are to be found some fine houses with considerable acres, although in a great many cases this has fallen over the years, for many reasons.

The Galbraith family originally came to Clanabogan from Scotland in the early 1600s. Having acted as Agents for the Earl of Belmore in Beragh and Sixmilecross in the 1630s, the family acquired the land at Clanabogan (boggy meadow) and in due course built 'New Grove' in 1809. The house was added to on several occasions and still remains occupied today.

In 1834, Samuel Galbraith offered £100 and an acre of land to the Bishop of Derry if he would allow him to present to the Curacy during his life. This was refused and the church was not built. It was not until 1861 that the Bishop agreed to the building of the church. It is dedicated to 'Christ Church' and made up of Drumragh in the Diocese of Derry and Dromore and Donacavey in the Diocese of Clogher.

In 1894 the Galbraith family had the east end redecorated. This work was entrusted to a well-known architect, Sir Thomas Drew. Drew chose the medium of marble, selecting it from Ireland, France and Italy. The result is most impressive for the visitor, especially the Mural Tablet by Sir Thomas Brock.

Hedge Schools and Mass Rocks are a relic of the severe Penal Era, and nearby at Corradinna is the best-known and most frequented mass rock in the district. It is tucked away in a secluded valley below the Pigeon Top with a stunning view over Omagh below. It was nearby at Cavancaw Upper in the 1980s that gold was discovered and efforts are ongoing to mine it in the future.

Mass Rock
CORRADINNA

It was a beautiful summer's day in August 1998 - Omagh was coming to the end of its Community Week when, on the Saturday afternoon, the children with their floats would converge on the town centre from the various community centres round the housing estates. Some of the floats were to have upwards of thirty children on them in fancy dress. This was one of the big cross-community ventures organised by the Omagh District Council during the summer months.

As a result, in the early afternoon the town began to fill up with parents and younger children coming to see the parade, due to start at 4 p.m. As is the custom in Omagh on Saturday afternoons throughout the year, the usual gathering of young people and teenagers had begun to meet and mingle. Of course the weekend shoppers from the surrounding rural areas were there, and also on this occasion, a group of children from Buncrana along with their Spanish friends from Madrid, who were attending an annual summer school in their town.

Following the Good Friday Agreement, the country was relaxed and enjoying a period of freedom from tension, shootings and bombings. However a maverick group had recently carried out bombings in Moira, Portadown and Banbridge, causing severe damage but with no loss of life. This group came to Market Street, Omagh, on August 15th, with a car bomb, which detonated at 3.08 p.m. in the area where the people had been advised to gather, following a misleading bomb warning.

The rest is history; 29 dead and over 300 injured, along with an inestimable number mentally scarred for life. The memorial garden is dedicated to their memory.

Flowers on Strule Bridge

People of Omagh

There is evidence of human habitation in Tyrone dating back to before 4000 BC. The first people would have been hunters and gatherers who, unfortunately, left little behind with which to identify them although tools dating from the Mesolithic era, which originated in Tyrone, have been found in the east of Ulster. Most archaeologists agree that it was c4000 BC that the first settlements were developed with the arrival of the first farmers in the area. This period is referred to as the Neolithic period and one of the earliest Neolithic farmsteads yet discovered in the British Isles is at Ballynagilly in Tyrone. It has been dated to about 3700 BC.

There is a wealth of archaeological evidence, including a hoard of Bronze Age ornaments found near Arboe, in the countryside surrounding Omagh which would suggest that our earliest forefathers were as attracted to the area as we are ourselves. The Ulster History Park at Cullion has recreated the earliest homesteads and affords the curious a glimpse of life in the country.

Those of a dry-boned scientific bent tell us that it was these early forefathers who first started to change the countryside which gradually evolved, through successive generations over the millennia to that which we now enjoy. Legend, however tells a different story. The area was the home and playground of giants such as Finn Mac Cool, whose games and contests helped to shape our surroundings. The historic hill of Knockmany, famed in song and story, and which was in the far distant past a royal burial place, is now preserved as an ancient monument. In legendary lore Knockmany was the centre and headquarters of the giants and fairies of Ulster and at the time the Giant's Causeway was under construction, Finn

People

McCool who was one of the workmen who lived on the tip-top of the hill. On one occasion a contest between two giants, Ermand Kelstach and Muckabaw for Finn's lovely red-haired daughter Granua was decided by throwing the shoulder-stone. This stone, it might be stated, was about the size and weight of a young mountain and the winner would be the contestant who from the top of Knockmany could throw the stone over the top of Bessie Bell - about half the width of Tyrone. Muckabaw had the first throw. The young mountain soared no doubt more or less like an atomic bomb - down the valley, over Seskinore, and struck the top of Bessie Bell, where the mark is still seen to the present day.

In the 5th century AD Christianity was imported to Ireland by St. Patrick and Tyrone has its sites which legend associates with the saint. The excavation of an extensive early Christian cemetery at Dunmisk has given us an interesting insight into the lives of our ancestors. Richard Ivens examined the contents of over 400 years and discovered that the average age of death was only 25; very few survived beyond the age of 40. So the old impression of life in the past as brutal and short would appear to have some basis. Perhaps as a result of the brevity of their lives the people appear to have been devout, and two of the best preserved Celtic Crosses in Ireland are to be found at Arboe and Donaghmore. Myths and legends abound in Tyrone like most parts of Ireland, and of course St. Patrick passed here as well.

Myths and legends about this early Christian period abound. At Lough Patrick, named after the saint, there was a fierce reptile that dragged horses, cows and other domestic animals into the lake when they went there to drink. St. Patrick destroyed the reptile, and established a church at the hill of Donaghanie, part of the ruins of which, together with the ancient cemetery, remain to this day.

Lough Patrick in the 19th century could be considered a mini-Lough Derg, since for one week-end in the summer months it became a place of pilgrimage where penitents would walk round the lake in their bare feet saying the rosary several times. Unfortunately, the weekend attracted undesirables with illicit liquor and all the trick o' the loop gambling games to relieve the pilgrims of their money. As a result, the clergy called a halt to the proceedings and, as time has passed, Lough Patrick has grown over.

From about the end of the 10th century the area surrounding Omagh fell within the kingdom of the kings of Cenel Eogain who ruled from Inishowen in the north, to Armagh in the south. The fort of Tullahogue is associated with these kings who were drawn from O'Neill family/clan and it was recorded as the traditional crowning place for the kings. The principal family in the area was the O'Hagan family who farmed most of the land and who traditionally took a prominent role in the coronation ceremony. Their family burial ground is at Donaghrisk, close to Tullahogue.

Very little is known of the early history of the town of Omagh; fire and sword have destroyed most of the ancient documents and records. What is known is that in early times Omagh was known by the names of Oigh-math, the seat of the Chiefs, but later it became Omey. The town grew up where the Drumragh and Camowen rivers join to form the Strule. It is clear that the early centuries of the past millennium were a turbulent time for Omagh and its environs. Turning to the Annals of the Four Masters, from 1459 to 1538 we find Omagh harassed by wars at regular intervals as the castle and town were fought over by competing sections of the O'Neill clan and the Anglo-Normans. In 1498 Mac Art O'Neill erected fortifications against the 'English' but on his defeat by the Earl of Kildare they were razed to the ground. The Earl of Kildare returned in 1509 and, so we are informed *"went unto the castle of the Oghmagh and it was taken by him...and the castle was broken down by the Earl after that and the Earl returned in triumph to his house from that expedition."* Mac Art O'Neill returned in 1512 and *"he builds in a week there the castle that had been broken down before that by the Earl of Kildare and leaves warders in it."*

People

This incarnation of the castle lasted only two years before it was destroyed by Art Junior. The last reference these Annals make to our town is dated 1538, when they say, *"Brien son of Niall O'Neill junior inrode on Niall, son of Conn to the castle of the Oghmagh, though there was peace and gossipred between them, and the castle was taken without warning and Niall himself, a great tale, was slain."*

In 1603 Lord Mountjoy, the Lord Deputy, having placed a garrison in Omagh under Sir Henry Dowra, inflicted a crushing defeat on the Earl of Tyrone, capturing the whole of his magazines, military chest and other valuables and causing him soon after to make his final submission at Mellifont. Chichester writing about Omagh or St. Omey as he calls it says, *"Round about this place there is great desolation, by reason of which it happeneth that merchants and other passengers weakly guarded travelling from Derric or liffer to the Pale are usually in their passage cut off and murdered."*

In 1609 the town and district was granted to Lord Castlehaven, but as he failed to erect a castle and settle the proper number of English on the land, as required by the terms of the grant, these lands reverted to the Crown and were given to Captain Edmund Leigh and his brothers John and Daniel. By 1611, Lord Carew was able to report, *"The Fort of Omye. Here is a good fort fairly walled with lime and stone about thirty feet high above the ground with a parapet, the river on one side and a large deep ditch about the rest; in which is built a fair house of timber in the English manner. Begun by Captain Edmund Leigh and finished by his brothers, at their own charge, upon the lands of the Abbey of Omye, at which place are many families of English and Irish, who have built them good dwelling houses, which is a safety and comfort for passengers between Dungannon and the liffer. The fort is a place of good import upon all occasions of service and fit to be maintained."*

There is an old map of about this date in the Library of Trinity College, Dublin, which shows this fort to the North of the town with its ramparts and cannon, but it is difficult to ascertain the exact spot on which it was built (thought to be in the area of the Kozy Korner). The town was surrounded by a wall or rampart and outside the southern gate the ruins of the old castle of the O'Neills is shown. The road to the Liffer and Derry crosses the river and then takes its way through swamps and bogs along the eastern bank of the Strule.

The Plantation of Ulster began in earnest under the Stuart kings but resistance was still strong. Charles I granted the manor of Arleston or Audleston (there is a house called Arleston on the Old Mountfield Road once occupied by a solicitor called King Houston; it is now Omagh District Council property), comprising 2,000 acres of land in and around Omagh, to James Mervyn in 1631, and some of this property is still in the possession of his descendants, the Archdales. When the great rebellion of 1641 broke out, Sir Phelim O'Neill marched against the castle which immediately surrendered and so escaped the terrible destruction which laid to waste the greater part of the country. In 1666 it

is said that there were only twelve householders in Omagh.

The year 1742 was a memorable one in the annals of the town, for in the May of that year a disastrous fire broke out and the whole town was destroyed, only the church (First Omagh on the Dublin Road) and two dwelling houses, one belonging to Mr. Hudson and the other to Mr. Christy, escaped the flames. The fire was accidental and is thought to have been caused by a careless chambermaid who was disposing of hot coals. All the old landmarks went and the town as it is today took shape out of the ashes.

The later half of the 18th century was an interesting one in the history of Ulster and Ireland as a whole. Encouraged by increasing economic prosperity, led by Henry Grattan the parliament in Dublin had been exercising a greater degree of independence from that in London. However, the rate of change was not enough for many especially in Ulster. The penal laws were applied against all who were not members of the established Church of Ireland

People

and the growing Presbyterian merchant class were frustrated by these petty restrictions. Many of their number had already emigrated to the north American colonies where they had taken a leading role in the war of independence. The declaration of independence was published by a Tyrone man, John Dunlap from Sixmilecross. Tyrone has provided the United States with three presidents to date, with the ancestral homes of Woodrow Wilson at Dergalt near Strabane; that of Ulysses S. Grant just outside Ballygawley at Dergina; and of James Buchanan at Deroran between Omagh and Beragh.

The people of Ulster where privy to the latest information as they received letters from relatives and the Belfast News Letter published the latest accounts. In fact because of the shipping routes from the colonies, Belfast often knew what was happening before London. From this period of revolutionary enlightenment grew the United Irishmen movement whose founders dreamt of political and economic independence for Ireland in which religious freedom would be guaranteed for all. This culminated in the doomed 1798 rebellion.

The 1798 rebellion didn't affect the Omagh area to any great degree, but the attack on Dundivin (Fintona Rectory - only recently demolished) is an interesting story. The account is naturally very subjective, as it comes from the pen of the Rev. William White of Ardess who was a friend of the family of the rector who so bravely defended Dundivin, the Rev. Johnston, Rector of Donaghcavey (1794-98). He described the Rev. Johnston, who built the fortress-like rectory at Dundivin, as *"a man of real piety, learning the talents, as well as of great courage and steady loyalty, but of remarkable eccentricity."*

As to Dundivin rectory, he says: *"It was about forty feet in length...... It was evidently built for defence, with only one entrance, projecting towers, forty portholes, and being provided with several stands of arms, was capable of making effectual resistance to any irregular attacking party."*

The account continues:- *"The disaffected sent him* (Rev. Johnston) *in the course of that year several messages desiring him to deliver up his arms and assuring him that if he complied they would not molest him. But he indignantly refused, and then they determined to obtain by force what they could not extort by fear. One evening, when the rest of the family was in bed and he, just on the point of retiring to rest, heard the distant barking of dogs which, continually becoming nearer and more distinctive, gave unequivocal proof of the approach of a large party of United Irishmen.*

He hastily summoned up a trusty man and a lad whom he had in the house. He placed the man on the staircase to defend the large window and the door, and took up his station in the larger room above in company with the lad whom he employed in loading the muskets for him. On his refusal to surrender, they poured excessive volleys from behind a turf stack which stood near the house, which he returned with undaunted spirit.....

The insurgents, finding they could make no impression by distant fire, at last ventured from their covert and, with a large sledge endeavoured to break open the door. But it was strongly secured by iron bars running across from post to post."

The corps of yeomanry was at that time on guard in the town of Fintona, and it may be asked why they did not hasten immediately to the assistance of their respected rector. The fact was that it was part of the insurgents' system to make false alarms in distant parts of the parish in order to draw off the attention of the yeomanry to those parts. Thus distracted and harassed, the corps, when they first heard the reports of the firearms on that evening, conceived it to be one of the usual feints, until the successive volleys assured them that the affair was serious. They hastened then where the sound directed them, to Mr. Johnston's house. But sometime before they reached it (for it was nearly two English miles distant) the gallant defenders had put their hundreds to flight - in fact, it is thought there were no more than thirty United Irishmen in the area at that time, hence the unlikelihood of the story being true.

People

The United movement in Tyrone was broken by a short reign of terror in 1798. Among those who protested against the 'severity' was Mr. Eccles, the local landlord.

A glimpse of the town at the beginning of the 19th century has been preserved for us by J. Gamble, and it shows the backward state of the country at that time. He found the streets dirty and irregular, and though there were some good houses, they were by no means as numerous as the others to which by no stretch of the imagination could this description be applied. He stayed at the Abercorn Arms Hotel (Super Valu today), known as 'Harkins'. When he asked the landlord about the history of the town he was told he was the only traveller who had ever made any enquiries about it. He concludes by saying, *"here is a degree of gloom about the town which is more easy to feel than to describe - if I were confined to a country town I would not choose Omagh"*. This was in 1810. When he revisited the town in 1819 he saw a great improvement and spoke in high terms of the cleanliness of the Inn.

Bell's Bridge was widened in 1819. Campsie Bridge was not built until 1836, so access to the other side of the river was not easy. It was not until some time after the erection of Campsie Bridge that 'Sandy Row' (Campsie Crescent) was built and the grander houses of Campsie Road began to appear towards the Swinging Bars. Up to the beginning of the twentieth century there were a number of thatched houses in High Street. Among the last to disappear were those on the sites now occupied by the Ulster Bank and the Tyrone County Club.

Omagh could boast a reading room in 1838, 'furnished with newspapers but not with periodicals or other literary works'. The News Room was still in existence in 1862. Perhaps this was the forerunner of the County Club which at first had its rooms in the White Hart Hotel. This hotel was a great feature of the town in olden days. Above the porch was a beautiful model of a white stag, 'couchant gardant' as the heralds would say. In its yard, when the Grand Jury was being sworn in, there might have been seen half a dozen coaches-and-four belonging to the leading gentlemen of the County. An old custom long survived, by which the hostler, who placed the skid under the wheel of the Judges' carriage going down the Court House hill, received half a sovereign for his pains.

The gaol in Omagh was built between 1814 and 1822 with stones from the quarries at Kirlish, Drumquin. An extension was erected between 1823 and 1825. This allowed the gaol to accommodate 300 prisoners under the care of fourteen keepers.

Of course, it's the hangings at any prison that interest the general public. Initially, executions were carried out on the Gallows Hill in the vicinity of New Brighton Terrace. Tradition has it that the gibbet was a tree to which a rope was attached. An unusual story links the gibbet to the new gaol, for the last man hanged on the Gallows Hill was the first man hanged in the new gaol. The individual was a horse thief from Fintona who was hanged on 'The Hill', but for some reason his friends whipped the body away before he was in fact dead. Sadly, he lived to

commit the same offense at a later date and this time no chances were taken and he was hanged in the new gaol.

The most sensational hanging was that of Thomas Hartley Montgomery, hanged at 8 a.m. on 26th August, 1873, for the murder of Newtownstewart bank cashier, William Glass, on 29th June, 1871. The irony of the case was that both men were close friends, and Montgomery initially was the police inspector who investigated that murder. The case created great press interest even in the 1870s, and later a Newtownstewart man, Brian McBride, wrote a play on the event, which was broadcast on several occasions. Another twist to the Montgomery story occurred after the gaol was closed and partially demolished in 1904. When work was being carried out, a rough coffin with the letter 'M' carved on it was discovered. It was thought to contain the remains of District Inspector Montgomery. The bones were divided up among the locals as souvenirs; the skull was given to Mr. Carson, the Crown solicitor and some of the bones to Colonel Irvine, the Sub-

People

Sheriff. It is said that up until recently the skull sat in a local solicitor's office and was used as an ashtray.

On an eminence close to the village of Seskinore stand the ruins of the old castle of Mullaghmore. The owner of the castle, and no doubt Master of the Hunt, in that far-away time, had an only child - a lovely maiden. A handsome and gallant young sportsman wooed and wed her. As a special item of entertainment for the wedding party, a meet of the Hunt was arranged. Immediately after the wedding the happy bridegroom and many guests set out for the fox covert in what is still known as 'The Old Cow Lane.' But the joy of the morning changed to sorrow in the evening: the bridegroom was thrown from his horse and killed.

The shock was too much for the lovely bride of but a few short hours; she lost her reason, and in the brief space of time before her death she found comfort from time to time in donning her beautiful white wedding dress. Then she would stroll down the Old Cow Lane in search of her beloved. Long after she was laid to rest, an old servant of the castle vowed that he had met the bride, arrayed in white, in the lane. Later, another old servant told a similar story, and there are those who, to the present day, maintain that the Lady of Seskinore still seeks her lost lover in the old lane.

There is nothing known of the history of the Black Bell of Drumragh, though from its resemblance and its similarity in construction to the Cumaseach bell of Armagh and several others of the same period, it must be supposed to date from the early 10th century.

The traditional keepers of the bell are the M'Enhills or McEnhills, and this is in accord with Irish usage, where famous bells have been preserved for centuries by different generations of the one family. They were entrusted with the safe-keeping of the sacred bell. They were accustomed to ring it at the funerals of members of the family, the oldest men carrying it before the coffin on the way to the church, and behind the coffin from the church to the graveyard.

The bell is now in the safe-keeping of the sacristan, Joseph Given, in the Sacred Heart Church, Omagh, where it can be viewed on request.

As befits an area with a long history of religious devotion Omagh has its fair share of places of worship. The Roman Catholic Chapel was in Gortinore, just beyond St. Lucia Barracks on the Derry Road; this was completely removed after another had been built in Brook Street in 1829. The present Chapel of the Sacred Heart was consecrated on 28th May, 1899. Completed a few years later when a second spire to St. Joseph was added.

The First Omagh Presbyterian Meeting House was built in 1721 on the site of the present Church House on the Dublin Road. The masonry work is said to have cost only £6.10s.0d. as the congregation provided the labour and materials. The present church, which was erected on the opposite side of the road, was opened on 30th May, 1897, and is a striking building constructed of local limestone, with

mouldings of red Ballochmyle sandstone imported from Scotland through the port of Derry. The old church was removed in 1998 and will be reconstructed at the Cultra Folk Museum.

The Second Omagh Presbyterian congregation built themselves a Meeting House at the other end of the town in 1752; this is the town's oldest surviving church, soon to be 250 years old. The Methodist Church was erected in 1857 on the site of a previous one which had stood there since 1811.

As Omagh was situated in the centre of a large agricultural district and its chief trade was in farm produce, it consequently possessed several markets. An archway led from the High Street into the Potato Market (opposite the Northern Bank) which also had an entrance from Bridge Street. Near Campsie Bridge was the Butter Market (roughly where the Travel Agency stands) and another archway led into the Flax Market (beside McIlveens). Here on Thursdays was held the Pork Market, and on Fair Days the

People

horses were sold here. At the other end of the town near the railway station was the Corn Market. The cattle fair was held on the first Saturday in each month on the Fair Green, which stretched from Kevlin Road to the top of Gallows Hill (behind Trinity Presbyterian Church). It occasionally overflowed into the streets, often along John Street as far as the Courthouse. Omagh has a recently-constructed large, modern cattle mart at Coneywarren, soon to be further developed for show and machinery exhibition purposes.

The half-yearly Hiring Fairs were held on the Saturday after the 12th of May and in October, and there were also quarterly fairs at Lamas and Candlemas. All the 'boys and girls' from far and near gathered on these days in the High Street to hire themselves out. A large contingent from Donegal, attracted by the higher wages obtainable in Tyrone, attended.

The town did not possess a Bank until the Provincial Bank opened a branch on 13th October, 1834. In March, 1836, it moved into its new premises. We are told that in 1838 *"the only manufacturers are those of tobacco and of ale and beer, of which latter there is an extensive brewery, the produce of which has acquired some celebrity"*. This brewery was built on the Gortin Road by Hans Peebles about 1820, where the present Scotts' Mills still stands today, and was purchased by William Scott in 1850.

The tobacco manufacturing was carried on by Edward Boyle at 17 Market Street, a house built by William Scott, and rope was made by Ann Collin on the Brookmount Road (still called the Rope Walk by some today). Opposite the rope works was a large coach factory owned by Wade.

The history of the middle of the 19th century in Tyrone as much as the rest of Ireland is dominated by the famine of the 1840s. The potato harvest of 1845 was badly affected by the blight and led to great but not total suffering. Those worse hit were in great want but it was not unusual for the harvest to partially fail and everyone was confident that the next crop would be healthy. It failed completely. Between

1846 and 1851 over 1 million deaths can be attributed to the effects of famine. The same number emigrated, a devastating blow to those left behind. To give an indication of the scale it should be stated that the population of Ireland in 1846 was recorded as eight and a half million, so by 1851 almost a quarter of the population had vanished. It is easy for those of us who have grown up with a comprehensive welfare state to condemn the official response to the crisis as totally inadequate and certainly it was condemned at the time. However official attitudes at the time as to the state's responsibility to its citizens was completely different and efforts were made through the existing support system to alleviate the suffering of the local population.

Prior to the famine most emigration had been voluntary, albeit in most cases driven by economic and political necessity. During the Great Famine it became funded by both the state and local landlords. In 1849 Edward Senior the Poor Law Inspector for the workhouses of Antrim, Armagh, Down, Londonderry and Tyrone recommended that the guardians of the workhouses should *"send as emigrants to Canada, at the cost of the Electoral Division, anyone of the able-bodied inmates of the workhouses, especially females... in this mode some of the permanent deadweight in the workhouse may be got rid of at a cost to the Electoral Division of about £5 or about one year's cost of maintenance."*

In addition to emigration the state also provided famine relief through the existing poor law structure and this was the time of the infamous soup kitchens and road building schemes. The latter being an indication of how entrenched was the 19th century view of the undeserving poor. Many of the roads built at this time can still be seen in Tyrone and the rest of Ireland today.

The year 1852 was an important one, for it was marked by an event of great consequence to the future prosperity of the whole town, namely the coming of the Dundalk, Enniskillen and Londonderry Railway, which was opened for

People

traffic on 13th September. In 1861 the Portadown, Dungannon and Omagh Junction Railway arrived at its terminus in Irish Town, where the goods station stood. Later these Companies were amalgamated and a line constructed joining the two stations. From that time on, the old stage coach passing on its way to or from Dublin and Derry was heard and seen no more. In order to facilitate the increasing amount of traffic between the station and the town, it became necessary to widen and improve what is now called John Street, and James Street was also enlarged about the same time. The arrival of the railways had a significant effect on the economy of the town and environs as Omagh now had a direct link with Dublin and Belfast and Derry and so goods could be exported and imported easily. From the coming of the railway the town really increased in size, with houses being built in great numbers on all roads leading out of the town.

It is important to remember that Omagh has been a garrison town since the 15th century, and as a result the names of many men and women who served in the wars of the 19th and 20th centuries are to be found on memorials throughout the areas where the Royal Inniskilling Fusiliers served. The Boer War Memorial on Drumragh Avenue was unveiled in the High Street in 1905 to the Inniskillings who died in the Boer War and other previous campaigns abroad. The Cenotaph on the Gortin Road or, as it should be properly called, the Tyrone War Memorial, was unveiled in October 1929 to the 2,000 war dead of Tyrone in the 1914-18 conflict. During WWII, over 300,000 British recruits were trained in Omagh. Some 7,000 8th Army U.S. G.I.s were stationed in and around Omagh prior to D-Day, and Generals Eisenhower and Montgomery met on several occasions in Knocknamoe Castle during the build-up to D-Day.

Ireland is a musical country, as the number of winning entries in the Eurovision Song Contest shows, along with the success of Riverdance in recent years. Omagh is no exception when it comes to music, drama and the arts. In the early part of the 20th century, all the dances were held in the Courthouse, and Joe Nugent and Annie Rooney both had dance orchestras which supplied the music.

During the war, several groups were formed to entertain the troops with music, singing and humour. Then in the late 1940s the Melody Aces were formed in Newtownstewart, and they started the modem trend towards the superb dance bands of the 1960s, which included The Plattermen, The Polka Dots, Brian Coll and the Buckaroos, Frank Chisum and the Pebbles, Derek and the Sounds, the Toreadors, and many more. There was a time when Omagh and district had more bands than any other town of its size in Ireland. One mustn't forget Jimmy O'Neill and the Swing Earls, formed during the war and spending most of their time in the Strand in Derry entertaining the troops.

Today, Brian Coll is still performing his Country and Western classics, while Artie McGlynn's guitar music is known nationwide. Elvis Presley lookalikes and singers are legend,

but few have the ability of Frank Chisum. Ray Moore, who once played with the Plattermen, now combines with his brother Bobby on keyboard and guitar - the Moores come from one of Omagh's most prolific musical families, with seven star instrumentalists to call from. Derek Mehaffey is a Cliff Richard lookalike without having to make the effort - he has turned his interests to gospel music with success at home and in the USA.

The best known of Omagh's singers today are Dominic Kirwan in the popular field, and Maureen Murphy in the classical field. Of course, the name that keeps Omagh top of the musical greats is Jimmy Kennedy, who was born in Pretoria Terrace on the Brookmount Road. His list of popular tunes during and after the war years is endless and include 'Red Sails in the Sunset', 'Harbour lights', 'The Teddy Bears' Picnic', and 'The Isle of Capri'. Finbar Wright, the Irish tenor, frequently ends his concerts with 'South of the Border Down Mexico Way'.

The district of Omagh has produced many

People

people who have excelled in many walks of life at home and abroad. Many went to England and the U.S.A., whilst the catholic clergy went to a wide variety of the under-developed countries of Africa and Asia as missionaries.

I have already mentioned the three presidents of the United States who had roots in Tyrone: Woodrow Wilson, Ulysses Simpson Grant and James Buchanan. Davy Crockett, of Alamo fame, had his roots in Castlederg, whilst a long list of poets and writers spring to mind; William Carlton born in Clogher on 26th February 1794; Alice Milligan, often referred to as the Nationalist/Republican poet; Rose Kavanagh of Kiladroy, who was born on 23rd June 1859 and attended the Loreto Convent; and Vincentia Rodgers of Ballynahatty, born in 1790. Living legends include writer Ben Kiely, poet John Montague - although born in New York has his roots in Garvaghey, Ballygawley; he wrote a most touching poem after the Omagh Bomb on 15th August 1998.

Other people in Drama, Art and Sport are playwright Brian Friel; star of the big screen and television, Paddy McElhinney; and Circuit of Ireland winner in 1964, Ronnie McCartney.

And so to the Omagh of recent times. Omagh is the largest town in the area with a population of over 20,000. It serves a wide farming community and is the main source of employment for the surrounding district. Emphasis is on dairying, with milk being processed at Nestle's factory on the Derry Road, Leckpatrick Dairy (Greengate) on the Tamlaght Road, and Strathroy Dairies near Cappagh. The meat plant at Doogary opened in the early 1970s and continues to grow in size, and two new advance factory sites have been developed nearby. Other well-known industrial employers are, Desmond & Sons on the Kevlin Road producing clothing; John Finlay (Engineering) at the Gortrush Industrial Estate (where many other smaller businesses are located); Woodlock Joinery at Killybrack (suppliers to the building trade and manufacturers of timber-framed homes); Strule fireplaces; and Scotts (Excelsior Mills) manufacturers of animal feeds.

There are many builders and building contractors working in the district as the town continues to grow in all directions. Administration is the largest employer in the area with the Western Health and Social Services Board (Sperrin Lakeland Trust) and the Western Education and Library Board, both situated on the Hospital Road. The D.O.E. (Roads Division) is located in the County Hall. There are two main hospitals - The Tyrone County Hospital and The Tyrone and Fermanagh Hospital. The Tyrone and Fermanagh Hospital is a psychiatric hospital which caters for both counties. The Sperrin Lakeland Trust has its offices at the hospital in the house previously occupied by the R.M.S. - Strathdene.

Omagh is well-catered for with regard to caring facilities, with a number of old people's homes, all of modem construction; Hillview, Springlawn, Gortmore, Knockmoyle, Drumragh, and Slieve Na Mon. Coneywarren on the Derry Road is for children up to 17 years of age. The Health Centre, opened in 1971, was the fourth and largest at the time in Northern Ireland, and provides all the G.P. services, including nursing and social, for the district.

There are two local newspapers: The Tyrone Constitution (founded 1844) and The Ulster Herald (founded 1900). Although not untouched by the Troubles, with the last and most devastating bomb being in 1998, the town has remained a vibrant and friendly place to visit with a wide selection of restaurants and hotels.

Most sports are catered for, both indoor and outdoor, from football and fishing to indoor bowls. The town has a good 18 hole golf course which is unique in that it is bisected by the main Dublin Road. The tennis club, founded in 1892, is the only one in Ireland playing on the same site continuously throughout both World Wars. Omagh Town Football Club plays in the First Division of the Football League, whilst the Rugby Club plays in the Fourth Division of the All-Ireland League. Horse-riding is popular, and several indoor equestrian centres are easily

People

accessed. The prize-winning Leisure Centre on the Old Mountfield Road has superb facilities for all ages, and two halls suitable for variety concerts with seating for up to 1,000 people.

The usual societies abound, giving the local population all-year-round choice, including water-skiing on the local lakes, sailing on nearby Lower Lough Erne, and sea sports off the coast of Donegal, one hour away. Many clubs and charity-raising societies exist to supply all tastes, both male and female - like chess, bridge, horticulture and photography. Again, there are several dramatic societies and, for those who like to sing, choral societies. Junior Chamber, Lions, Round Table and Rotary are all available, whilst the ladies have the Women's Institute, Inner Wheel, Ladies Circle and the Soroptomists.

The District Council offices are situated in a modern building in Grange Park since 1978. The town is twinned with Hayes de Roses, a town near Paris.

The town has excellent primary schools and three grammar schools. The grammar schools are The Academy, The Loreto Convent, and The Christian Brothers. There are also two secondary intermediate schools; Omagh High School and The Sacred Heart College for Boys and Girls, and an Integrated College.

The bomb which exploded with such devastating effect on 15th August ripped the heart out of Omagh. The town is rebuilding its wrecked shops and offices, but rebuilding the bodies and minds of those injured will be a much longer process. It has been a most difficult time for many, but the various organisations set up to cope with all eventualities are now in place, and no-one need feel isolated or that they do not have someone to turn to when they feel down and depressed, as they undoubtedly will following the loss of loved ones in such a horrific and tragic manner. Thanks to the good people of this island and beyond, much encouragement has been given to help the people of Omagh look to the future with confidence.

Sources

Tombstones of the Omey - William McGrew

North-West Ulster - Alistair Rowan

A Book of Christmas Poems and Others - Thomas Strain

Prospect of Tyrone - Mary Rodgers

Old Fintona - P. O'Gallachair

Poems of Alice Milligan - Henry Mangan

History of the Parish of Drumragh - Rev. D.F. McCrea, MIRA

The Ulster American Folk Park - History

Townland Names of County Tyrone - P. McAleer

Clanabogan Parish Church - Rev. T.W. Benson, MA

A Hundred Years A-Milling

Selected Poems - Robert Kerr

Old Dromore - P. O'Gallachair

Lisnamallard - Richard Scott

Cappagh Parish Magazines

Drumragh Parish Magazines

Ulsterheart - Rev. Brett Ingram

Drumquin Series - Patrick Scully

The Official Guide to Omagh and District

The Omagh Business Directory

The Dill Worthies - Rev. James Reid Dill, MA

A History of the Parish of Ardstraw West and Castlederg - Philip Donnelly

Newtownstewart Remembered - William Dunbar

Images of Omagh and District - C.J.H. Mitchell

Meetings and Memories in Lower Badoney

The Gate Lodges of Ulster - J.A.K. Dean

Acknowledgements

I would like to thank everyone, especially Jane O'Donnell, Mildred Scanlon and Nina Leech for their assistance while I was working on the collection of paintings for this book and hope it is worthy of their kind efforts.- William M. Park

My thanks and best wishes to Eileen Logan and Angus Mitchell for all their help during this project - Dr. Haldane Mitchell

Dear Reader

We hope you have enjoyed this book. It is one of a range of illustrated titles which we publish. Other areas currently featured include:–

Cottage
Publications

Strangford Shores	Donegal Highlands
Dundalk & North Louth	Drogheda & the Boyne Valley
Armagh	The Mournes
Belfast	Fermanagh
Antrim, town & country	Ballynahinch & The Heart of Down
Inishowen	South Donegal

**Cottage Publications
15 Ballyhay Road
Donaghadee, Co. Down
N. Ireland, BT21 0NG**

Also available in our 'Illustrated History & Companion' Range are:-

Coleraine and the Causeway Coast	City of Derry
Lisburn	Banbridge
Ballymoney	Holywood

We can also supply prints, individually signed by the artist, of the paintings featured in the above titles as well as many other areas of Ireland.

For the more athletically inclined we can supply the following books from our illustrated walking book series :-

Bernard Davey's Mournes   Tony McAuley's Glens

For more details on these superb publications and to view samples of the paintings they contain, you can visit our web site at **www.cottage-publications.com** or alternatively you can contact us as follows:-

Telephone: +44 (028) 9188 8033   Fax: +44 (028) 9188 8063